T0105683

No One to Tell, Someone to Care

JOYCE LANDRUM

WESTBOW
PRESS
A DIVISION OF THOMAS NELSON

Copyright © 2012 by Joyce Landrum.

All rights reserved. No part of this book may be used or reproduced by any means, graphic, electronic, or mechanical, including photocopying, recording, taping or by any information storage retrieval system without the written permission of the publisher except in the case of brief quotations embodied in critical articles and reviews.

WestBow Press books may be ordered through booksellers or by contacting:

WestBow Press
A Division of Thomas Nelson
1663 Liberty Drive
Bloomington, IN 47403
www.westbowpress.com
1-(866) 928-1240

Because of the dynamic nature of the Internet, any web addresses or links contained in this book may have changed since publication and may no longer be valid. The views expressed in this work are solely those of the author and do not necessarily reflect the views of the publisher, and the publisher hereby disclaims any responsibility for them.

Certain stock imagery © Thinkstock.
Any people depicted in stock imagery provided by Thinkstock are models, and such images are being used for illustrative purposes only.

ISBN: 978-1-4497-4181-5 (sc)
ISBN: 978-1-4497-4180-8 (e)

Library of Congress Control Number: 2012903702

Printed in the United States of America

WestBow Press rev. date: 03/28/2012

Contents

To my church family including our pastor, my husband,

God bless you all!

Foreword

"Verily, verily, I say unto you, Except a corn of wheat fall into the ground and die, it abideth alone: but if it die, it bringeth forth much fruit." **John 12:24**

King James Version (KJV)

Joyce had everything going for her: A great husband, three wonderful children and nine beautiful grandchildren. She had put herself through college as an adult and was well loved as a schoolteacher. Her husband pastored a thriving church and she was a beloved Sunday School teacher. She was a sought after teacher for women's retreats. She was healthy and always "on the go"!

And God had a preparation for Joyce. In a story that would, in some ways, rival Job's it seemed that each aspect of her life came unraveled. She developed severe back pain. Surgeries were not successful in eliminating her pain. Over time, and with much grief, she realized that she could no longer stand the physical demands of teaching. As her life quieted and the demands lessened, she found herself pulling in. Her energy level fell. Some days she didn't leave home. While she still clearly loved her children and grandchildren, sometimes they felt like more demand than blessing. She didn't always feel like teaching her Sunday School class. Sometimes she could not even bring herself to go to church. Her health failed in many ways. She began to not even recognize herself.

She had remembered her mother as very difficult and had worked to make peace with the complicated feelings her mother stirred. One day she had the horrible realization that the very one she had idolized had sexually molested her for much of her childhood, only stopping when she reached puberty. She struggled to know who she was in this context. She was devastated.

Along this painful, difficult path she, one day, lost her will to live. It was during a psychiatric hospitalization that she met God in a new way. She gave her heart to Him anew. Thus began a path back to health.

These poems represent Joyce's expression of her pain, her loss and her hope. It is my belief that God is doing a great and difficult work in her; a work that will "bringeth forth much fruit."

Others will find comfort, encouragement, and challenge in Joyce's poems. She tells the story of faith lived out when life is very hard. God's love shines through.

Introduction

I'm looking back right now; looking back almost three years. Did I think I would ever be the victim of sexual abuse? Did I ever imagine it had already happened and I didn't remember it? No! Now I'm two and a half years down the road since remembering the abuse that lasted from the ages of four through twelve. I don't know when I repressed the memories but they lay buried until five months after my sixtieth birthday. I've been told that God took them to protect me and returned them to me when He felt I was ready to handle what had happened to me as a child. I didn't feel ready then and I still don't feel ready.

I am trying to learn how to put my life back together and how to trust again. I finally realize the only way to heal is to give my hurt and pain to God. This is so hard. When do I think I'll be okay—never completely. When do I think I will be back to "normal"—there is no normal.

There is one thing I am realizing; the devil meant this for evil but God can make it turn out for good. God is using the events of my past. He is arming me with the ability to share my story. Maybe it will help someone; maybe it will help me. I don't know but I finally have hope and I trust God completely. These events shall not be in vain . . .

September, 2009

"Some Day"

All around me people go their way
They have no idea I am not okay.
I hide it so they cannot see
I must not expose this real me.

The real me is so sad to behold
The real me has scars new and old.

All inside me is turmoil and pain
No one knows I have thoughts of disdain.
I cover it most all of the while
But sometimes it slips out, bitter bile.

The real me is so sad to behold
The real me has scars new and old.

But someday I've the promise from God
Maybe from a blink or a nod.
He'll tell me to let you all see
He has healed me, I'm now a new me.

Then the real me will have sweet release
Then the real me will know true peace.

September, 2009

"My God"

Down in the depths of despair
I search for a reason to care.
Then I look deeper still
Suddenly, I see someone so real!

It is God who has come all the way
It is God who has turned my night to day.

Then I know I shall be able to live
I will even have something to give.
I look into the scars of my past
And find all the love that He hast.

It is God who has come all the way
It is God who has turned my night to day.

I look forward to healing and peace
And just maybe for the hurting to cease
For my God has come all the way
And my God has given back my day.

September, 2009

"Depression"

The lowness comes in like a thief
It stays; I get no relief.
The hurt and the pain
The guilt and the blame,
Depression is its name.

The thoughts to do myself harm
Are distorted and cause me alarm.
The ways and the means
So easy it seems
Depression, how it clings.

The exhaustion and pain left behind
The horrors now crowding my mind
But wait, a voice sweet sublime
He says, "I was there all the time."

September, 2009

"Us"

My darling quiet little girl
My finding, this wondrous rare pearl!
You shielded me and hid me too
You did all a little girl could do.

For to know God's love and His grace
We had to come to this place.

Then Emme stepped into our life
She heard all the bitterness, the strife.
She shielded you and me just the same
She protected us from his sick game.

For to know God's love and His grace
We had to come to this place.

Now I know both of you, part of me
It's time for us to find the key.
I'll open the door to our pain
We'll see none of it was in vain.

For to know God's love and His grace
We had to come to this place.

September, 2009

"Black Hole"

When I fall into that big black hole
I am so surprised it has happened again.
To find my way out is my next big goal
And I determine not to go back where I've been.

When I finally creep out to see daylight
I am so amazed at the feat I've just done.
I've climbed and scratched with all my might
This battle is over but is the war won?

Because each time I think it is all past
There can't be more or I won't survive.
I think, "This is it, I'm well at last"
And then at that moment the world takes a dive.

Over and over the scene will replay
I'm in, I'm out, I'm up, I'm down.
My soul and my body and my mind must pay
And tomorrow it'll just be another round.

How can this be? How'd this happen to me?
I'm over 60 and always the solid one
I'm the one who helps everyone else you see.
But this time, nothing works, nothing gets done.

New drugs, new doctors, new suggestions to try
I pray, how I pray, something will put me on track.
No sleep, too much sleep, tons of tears I cry
But grasping the hope someday I'll be back.

September, 2009

"I Am the One"

The sadness creeps in like a fog
It envelops, it surrounds, it clouds;
All it touches, it enshrouds.

I am the one in the middle
I am the one it belittles.

The sadness stays and empties me out
It sucks, it drains, it paralyzes
All that it finds, it compromises.

I am the one it drains
I am the one it defames.

Finally the sadness creeps away silently
It has done its job for this day
And that which is left is enough, I pray.

I am the one left searching to find
I am the one trying to take back my mind.

September, 2009

"Once Upon A Time"

Once upon a time, I was healthy
Once upon a time, I was free
Once upon a time, I was sane
Once upon a time, I loved life
Once upon a time, I had a career
Once upon a time, I had energy
Once upon a time, I made money
Once upon a time, I respected myself.

Once upon a time!

Once upon a time, people asked me for advice
Once upon a time, I had a Sunday School class
Once upon a time, I was a public speaker
Once upon a time, I was taken seriously
Once upon a time, I counseled others
Once upon a time, I babysat grandchildren
Once upon a time, I taught a 4th grade class
Once upon a time, I trusted myself.

Once upon a time!

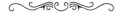

September, 2009

"The Value"

The value of a life is measured by what it can do for another.
The value of a life is measured by how far it can go for another.
The value of a life is measured by how high it can climb for another.
The value of a life is measured by how open its arms are for another.
The value of a life is measured by how freely its heart opens for another.
The value of a life is measured by how hard it fights to return to normal.
The value of a life is given by God and cannot be taken away.
I have value!

September, 2009

"45 Hours"

As I entered the ward the door slammed behind me.
I had been locked in a world unknown to me.
Suddenly with my eyes seeing clearly,
I realized freedom just wasn't to be.

I was only given the basics—soap, cream and toweling.
No one inquired about my fear and my pain.
The door remained locked; my goings recorded
No one heard my heart loudly howling.

Then I cried, "God, help, all is lost!"
He was just waiting to hear me ask.
I gave up my control and my strength
He offered me everything; no cost.

It's unmerited favor and grace is its name.
Unconditional love is given then too.
The most horrific 45 hours of my life
But in a moment a new person I became.

I've been transformed by His glorious grace
I'm singing about His love and His care.
Each day gets sweeter; more precious to live
Thank you, God; my life is no longer a waste.

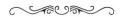

September, 2009

"This Stupid Hospital Bed"

Today just happens to be the worst of my life
As I sit in this hospital bed all alone.
I feel I am made of just sawdust & bone
Nothing left of my heart, it has crumbled and gone.

I tried for months to cure myself
I worked so hard every day.
I read, and I wrote, I even tried to pray
And in the end it just twittered away.

Now here I sit in this hospital bed
What will I say to them now?
Will I tell them I just couldn't cope with it all?
Will I tell them I'm worth nothing no how?

She probably knew what she was talking about
When she said I was stupid in the head.
For look where I ended up at the end of the day
In this stupid hospital bed.

October, 2009

"Too Much to Process"

The little girl was innocent and pure
Then he came along and much he made her endure.
He lied to her and hurt her deeply
But God never left her, of that I'm sure.

Emme lost him because he walked away
So weird, she actually wanted him to stay.
No words, no looks, no love was given
I prayed for him to come back someday.

Now I'm a grandmother, yet still a child
I just found out, I've only known for a while.
How do I process the hurt and the pain?
How do I get rid of the bitterness and guile.

October, 2009

"God Alone Will Do"

In January I lost my health
I learned to lean on others.

In February I lost my hope
I learned others held me up.

In March I lost my independence
I learned I had never been alone.

In April I lost my worship
I learned trust could help it return.

In May I lost my way
I learned it was God's way I needed.

In June I lost my will to survive
I learned He would carry me each day.

In July I lost my joy
I learned He had more to give.

In August I lost my fight with myself
I learned that was how I could live.

In September I lost my freedom to choose
I learned You know the best plan for me.
And now I'm waiting for it all to come back
Because I've just learned all I need is You!

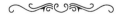

October, 2009

"God Stands"

God stands ready to take my burden
God stands ready to shoulder my cares.
If only I can learn to trust Him fully
If only I can learn to leave them there.

God stands ready to restore my joy
God stands ready to calm my fear.
If only I can learn to take my hands off me
If only I can learn to consider Him dear.

God stands ready to carry my load
God stands ready to soothe my pain.
If only I can learn to call out His name
If only I can learn His promises to claim.

God stands ready to guide me now
God stands ready to answer my call.
If only I can learn to let Him lead
If only I can learn not to put up walls.

God stands ready to answer my prayers
God stands ready to dry each of my tears.
If only I can learn to cry out to Him
If only I can remember He's always near.

October, 2009

"Clean"

I watched the rain as it fell today,
It hit the trees, the ground and the creek.
As the drops hit they all seemed to say
We're washing your soul, is this what you seek?

My soul responded, "I've been washed clean,"
The blood of Christ took care of it all.
Now He wants me to learn to always lean
So each time I stumble He can break my fall.

I'm struggling to learn this new way of life
To let Him take care of my woes.
To hand Him over my worries and strife
To let Him conquer my foes!

It's hard to learn this new plan of His.
I've always done it on my own.
But the truth of it all really just is
It's so nice not to be all alone!

October, 2009

"Laughter Lost"

This room I'm in is for little boys.
There are shelves of toys and books.
It looks like who plays here knows real joy
Cause there's things in all the crannies and nooks.

There's pictures too, lots of them around
Of grandmas, and grandpas galore.
I can almost hear a chuckle of a sound
If I listen just outside the door.

But I'm in here now and the chuckles die down.
No children giggling, just silence; it's deafening too!
Not one laugh, not one single sound
To bring it back, what can I do?

October, 2009

"Once In A While I Feel Like Me"

Once in a while I feel like me
But not very often you see
Cause I've been to the other side of hell
And it's taken a toll too hard to tell.

Once in a while I feel like me
But usually I don't have the key
To opening the locked up joy within
And finally claiming this war a win.

Once in a while I feel like me
Once in a while I can just be
But most of the time I'm nowhere near
I'm huddled in a closet of fear.

Someday, somehow I'll feel like me
I'll wake up and know who I am.
I will have discovered the key
All along it was to behold the Lamb.

October, 2009

"Not Him, Please"

My heart is broken, my heart is numb
I just remembered you hurt me.
I almost feel as though I will succumb
I will fade away and no longer be.

You know, I loved you, I trusted you too.
You took it and twisted it all up.
You changed from my hero to my foe
You drained me, you made love corrupt.

My heart is broken, my heart will heal.
God has cradled me in His care.
He has a plan for me, His will
If only I trust Him, If only I dare.

God loves me so much, He gives me grace.
He will sustain me through this time.
Whatever is before me, whatever I face
He will help me as I make this climb.

October, 2009

"Collapsed World"

My world as I knew it has just collapsed
It just crumpled and fell all apart.
How could this be my family?
Where do I pick up, where do I restart?

I restart with God guiding me through
I trust Him to build me back.
For He's been with me since I began
He'll protect me and provide every lack.

I'm stronger now than I was before
Because I've realized I'm not alone.
My Lord and my God, my dearest friend
The best thing, for my sins He did atone.

I trusted Christ on that September night
I took my hands off my own life
I asked God to take over the job
To heal all my hurt and strife.

It will take a while with this new news
I don't think I've taken it in.
I think I'm numb on the inside and out
But I know I'll be well again!

October, 2009

"Dear God"

Dear God, thank you for coming into my life.
Thank you for staying so close to me.
Thank you for letting me lean
Thank you, your care I now see.

Dear God, without you I would be dead.
Without you I'd have met my fate.
For there were many times I wanted to die
But you encouraged me to wait.

Dear God, please help me through this terrible time.
This time when I feel stripped bare
These days when I'm numb and so dumbstruck
Show me your love and your care.

October, 2009

Written in church on a Wednesday evening

"In Christ's Arms"

My Lord and my God, He loves me so
From the top of my head to the tip of my toes.
I finally let go and called out to Him
He answered immediately and He came in.
He filled my heart with His wonderful grace
Forever from now He will plead my case.
His love unconditional and always abounding
His word everlasting and loudly resounding.
To all who will listen and open their heart
He waits in the wings His grace to impart.
Stop trying to do everything just "right"
Shout out to Him and live in the light.
For try as you might you work more and more
But in Christ's arms, the effort is 'oer!

November, 2009

"Me"

I hurt
I cry
I moan
I die
I rage
I sigh
I rant
I cry
I write
I drive
I stay
I ask why
I cry
I cry
I cry!

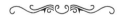

November, 2009

"My Depression"

The hours tick by and I cannot sleep.
My mind keeps returning to the deeds
he did to us.
I'm afraid they're in my heart for keeps.

Emme was so angry at what she saw
And the fact that he just calmly walked away.
He ignored them both; that should have been good
But instead it's left a wound that's so raw.

We didn't remember the pain
But the damage was there still the same.
No self-love, no confidence at all
Everything in life was all loss, no gain.

Finally, it all came to a head, depression in full force.
It holds me tightly in it's firm grasp.
I remember it all and it seems so unreal.
Maybe I can get well;
Now that God has shown me the source.

November, 2009

"Today"

Today, my soul dipped back in time
To the days of despair and gloom.
To thoughts so dark they seen unreal
They are all about blackness and doom.

Today, my heart almost broke in two
Thinking about all the times with him.
Not remembering all those years ago
Now knowing and feeling so grim.

Today, my brain became numb to it all
It was just too much to endure.
Eight years of abuse then more of neglect so complete
The rest just muddled and obscure.

Today, my body aches to feel normal again
To laugh, to work, to enjoy and do.
To know that I'm doing normal things
To know my lapses are few.

Today, my innermost being responds
God is working all my hurts to alieve.
He is drying my tears, singing to me
A complete act of grace I receive!

November, 2009

"Long Days"

What a long day I've had today!
It stretched on for hours and hours.
It broke into sadness and deep unrest
It certainly was not my best.

At church this morning I felt overwhelmed
I looked around at all the faces there.
I knew all wished for my return
I knew all showed great concern.

This afternoon I slept a while and it helped.
I awoke to find my fear had returned.
Mike had left for church and I was all alone
That was a circumstance I could not condone.

I texted and no one responded to my need
Then as I panicked and continued to wait,
I realized God was speaking to me.
He whispered, "I am so very near."

Then suddenly three friends knocked on the door
God sent them bounding in to help.
They uplifted my spirit and made it soar
They reminded me what friends are for.

November, 2009

"Don't Give A Rip"

When I say I don't give a rip
I think I'm just trying to forget.
All the pain, all the torment to me,
All the days when I couldn't just be.

I am trying to block myself off to the pain
I am trying to make it thru each day.
I want to just wake and live my life
I only want an end to this strife.

And then there's the anger within my heart
The anger at both of them.
The absolute combustible, blazing fire
That within my soul never dies.

Finally there's the newness that struggles to breathe
To get out of the confines it is in.
To heal all the ugliness, sorrow, and pain
and know none of this was in vain.

November, 2009

"Anger"

I need to get this anger out
This poison that dwells in my bones
That tries to take over my heart
God says, "Easy, let it through!"

I need to get this anger out
It takes me over and it stays
It makes me forget I have a clean soul
God says, "Easy, I am with you."

I need to get this anger out
Get it out for once and for all
Get rid of it and replace it right now
God says, "Easy, I'm here and I won't go."

November, 2009

"Him"

Shame for it all, but none from him
Exiled to a place unknown.
eXuded poison from his flesh
Until it was transferred to me.
Alluding him became my quest
Lonely, absent, I do not exist.
Loving, there was none in that place
Yearning and searching for escape.

All is lost, no escape from him
Being me, I've no idea who I am.
Unable to stop him, unable to breathe
Seeing him made my heart stop.
Ended, thank God it's over now
Dealing with the scars, forevermore!

November, 2009

"One Day"

One day I looked and there was no me.
The pictures were of some little girl.
She was shy, she was scared, she was so young
But as I looked I wondered who could she be.

One day I looked and there was just me
They had all disappeared from my view.
They'd been so cruel, so abusive and sick
No wonder my heart couldn't see.

One day I looked and there was just a shell
All the parts that made me up had gone.
They had been used up and discarded by them
Maybe this is what it's like in hell.

One day I looked and there was no me
I had tried so hard to save some part.
I had worked, and struggled and cried and prayed
But alas! It just couldn't be.

November, 2009

"The Puzzle"

Life is so confusing to me right now
I am so very weary of trying to live.
I have done everything I've been asked to do
But I'm at the point now, I just know nothing, no how!

I don't know how to pull myself up.
I don't know how to start over again.
I don't know how to stop all the pain.
I don't know how, please interrupt.

If you know what I could do to rise
If you know what I am suffering from.
If you know what else may come
If you know what, Please no lies.

Yes, life is hard, life's hurts are compelling
I'm struggling, and pushing and pulling.
Maybe there's something else I could do
I sure hope so, my heart is rebelling.

November, 2009

"I Belong in this World"

I am so proud to be improved
I've worked to get better and strong.
I'm processing all the past horrors
I'm learning just where I belong.

I belong in this world, just where I am.
I am a mother, a wife
I am a teacher, a patient, a friend
But for sure I am God's child and He is my life!

This journey I'm on is hard and long
I encounter so many bumps along the way.
But I'm getting stronger as I go
I'm improving with each passing day.

Soon a year will have come and gone
A year I've considered to be lost.
But now I'm reconsidering that thought
The growth may just be worth the cost.

December, 2009

"Sunny Skies"

Sunny skies, gloomy eyes
Lizards dashing, Joyce bashing.
Kids playing, Bing crooning.
In the midst of beauty
I sit here feeling guilty.

Why? Because I'm me.
Why? Because I can't just be.
What? Taking a nosedive.
Where? Into the abyss of my mind.
Where? Into the chains that bind.
How? I take me there.
How? I leave myself bare.
When? For the rest of my life.
When? Til the end of this strife.

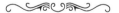

January, 2010

"No Sleep"

Hey, where'd you go, Sleep?
I need you so much tonight.
I have big plans in store
I want to make sure I do them right.

Hey, when you comin' back, Sleep?
I been waiting for quite a while
I've written and read and thought
Now I'm staring at the clock dial.

Hey, why can't I keep you Sleep?
You know I love to snooze
But you go away and stay so long
I'm sure some brain cells I'll lose.

Hey Sleep, what if you don't come?
I'll be sad and sick and weary
I need to know I can get rest
A good eight hours is the theory.

Well Sleep, I'm ordering you to come!
I won't have it any other way
Life's too short, and sleep too sweet
I don't want to miss another day.

Okay Sleep, this is my last plea—
Come now and make my eyes stay shut.
Ah wait, I do think I'm going but wait . . .
Now it's time to get up.

December, 2010

"God Can"

One, two, life just crashed
Three, four, please no more
Five, six, can it be fixed?
Seven, eight, not at this late date
Nine, Ten, Oh yes He can!

"Battle For Sanity"

Roses are red, daisies are white
This year I will continue the fight.

"Ruthless Tactics Thwarted"

The enemy has one desire—ruin me
The Savior has one desire—save me
I have one desire—trust God!

December, 2010

"Trusting God"

I tried to trust God for the rest of time
I was unable to fight that long.
Then I read try "Moment to Moment"
And low and behold that worked fine.

I tried to trust God for the rest of time
I had made it moment to moment.
So I decided I'd try "Hour to Hour"
And guess what? I made it mine.

Tomorrow I will try "Day to Day"
Leaning on Him all the while.
I'll trust Him to cover me, hide me, and love me
It'll work because I'm God's child.

December, 2010

"Christmas"

Today is the day we celebrate the birth of God's Son.
Of course there's other ado and fuss.
Shopping and cooking and traveling too,
To be with loved ones, oh what fun.

I fear many forget the true meaning of this day
And it may be that I am among that lot.
Shopping and cooking and running too,
To make it so special I say.

Jesus, the Christ, the ultimate sacrifice
Help me to think on this Holy night.
Living and suffering and dying for me
To make it possible, He paid the price.

God, I love you and want to trust you fully.
Please remove the barrier that seems to have grown
Hurting and dwelling and remembering the pain
To make it I give it to You daily.

December, 2010

"Moving On"

Last week I spoke to all the ladies of the church
I had waited for just the right time.
In my heart I had to search
Through the trouble and pain I had to climb.

I told my story of depression and abuse
Received as a child so undeserving.
It began a great battle, with a possibility to lose.
It's not over yet, it's just beginning.

Now it's time to write my book
I want no more hurt, just closure for me.
I want God to give me that loving look
That tells me, my child I see.

He sees that the book had to be written
To open the sores and drain the poison.
All the small places that were hidden
He opened and brought them out in the open.

So now maybe I'll be able to move on
Serving and loving and helping others too.
At church, at school, as I look beyond
To do His will and help, is what I want to do.

December, 2010

"The Day"

December 25th is the day
That Jesus Christ made the way.
By paying the price He had to pay
And on that cross He had to stay.

December 25 is the day
We celebrate, hoopla is okay.
But, our lives, we remember who paid.
Dear Lord, thank You, we pray.

December 25th is the day
Giving is a central theme we say.
But sometimes we see it all fray
And turn into turmoil, dismal and gray.

So, remember December 25th, the day
Of all days to thank Him, Hurray!
By loving and giving and trusting okay
For there's nothing greater, no way!

December, 2010

"Words"

Some words I'm still struggling with
I'm working so hard to understand.
Maybe that's the problem
I must learn to put it in His Hands.

First there's grace, boy, was that one tough
I'd never experienced such love.
God's riches paid by Christ for me
You sent it swiftly from above.

The next one was mercy, true and giving
The greatest example, of course, was God.
He tended and nurtured me all along
He showed me true love, true living.

The final one was trust, I tried to get it
I missed it at the beginning.
I didn't know it wasn't mine to conquer
He offered and I just had to receive it.

December, 2010

"Life is Strange"

Life is strange don't you think?
You're sailing through on a whim
When suddenly you hit a bump in the road
And nothing is the same ever again.

Life is strange don't you see?
Upon first glance all seems well
Then with intensity you look again
And realize you're injured, you fell.

Life is strange don't you feel?
Your subconscious hides the hurt.
You think you are happy and oh so content
But what you feel inside is like dirt.

Life is strange don't you know ?
God can take the dirt and make you clean.
He washes you as white as snow
So as His witness you now can beam.

Life is strange, life is grand
God can take the sadness and give bliss.
He can rebuild and make us beautiful for Him
And for time and eternity I am His.

December, 2010

"Taking the Time to Heal"

One year went by and now another one too
I never dreamed it would last this long.
So many days spent being sad and blue
I never thought my life could go so wrong.

In September 2009 I was locked in a unit
In total despair and wanting to die.
There were good days and bad days with me in the middle
There were tears every day, with every word a sigh.

In April 2010 I was suicidal again
I ended up at Focus by the Sea.
New meds, new doctors, support groups too.
There should be a way to get better
But no one could find the key.

Now, in one more day I'll enter a new year
Perhaps it will be a time of healing.
Maybe God will bring to a close the heartache and fear
The answer God's given me is kneeling.

Kneeling and praying and trusting Him day by day
Reading the Bible about his mercy and grace.
Allowing the potter to mold me like clay
Searching and finding peacefulness in this place.

Yes, a long time has passed with much grief and pain
Much time spent in pursuit of peace.
So much has been lost, now it's time to regain
It's time for the chaos to cease.

I'm trusting you, God, Your love I'm feeling
You want what was meant for evil to be good.
I'm praying and reading and striving to be
A Christian who just keeps kneeling!

January, 2011

"God is the Only One"

God, I'm lying in the bed feeling oh so low.
God, Please lift me up, help me to know.

I know You've watched me the whole of my life
You've hidden me beneath Your wings in times of strife.

Sometimes I haven't known you were even there
Because I tangled up myself, thinking only I cared.

I've read so many books to try to help me so
But I haven't spent as much time in the Bible, now I know.

I know Your word is a lamp unto my feet
I know it with every time my heart takes a beat.

Why I don't pick it up more is a puzzle to me
Could it be the enemy yet again, is that part of the key?

Well, listen to me you old deceiving face
You will not take any more of my space.

You've taken enough for a lifetime and more
You've stolen my happiness and left me poor.

Go away, stay away, you're not welcome here.
Go away, stay away, God is the one who's dear.

January, 2011

"Trust"

Oh my, I've been so confused and torn
I didn't develop the trust I needed.
But God knew it all and never left my side
Each time I called Him, He heeded.

I've cried and prayed and pondered it all
I've "leaned on my own understanding."
I've not trusted in Him with all my heart
But He wouldn't give up, He kept demanding.

Now the day has come, I trust Him so.
I'm frightened, shyly believing His word.
My precious God I see your plan now;
I came, I listened, I heard.

Trust; I'm beginning to see it all
God is opening my heart day by day.
I'm choosing to let God control my life
His is the only way.

Trust, the hardest journey of my life
I was so afraid to take that step.
And there are still many steps ahead
But each promise so far He's kept.

January, 2011

"From Blaming to Thanking"

I blamed You God for letting it happen
I questioned You for not protecting me.
I discounted You for not stepping in sooner
I resented You too, for not making him see.

I blamed myself for not yelling out loud
I hated myself because he ruined what I had.
I held myself accountable for all the pain
I never told a soul, I was too, too sad.

Now I see, You had my back
You protected me for all these years.
I thank you profusely with all my heart
Now with joy I shed these tears.

Will I continue to have trouble and sadness?
Yes, along the way they will come.
I'll need Your reminders, dear sweet God
I'll need Your touch when I'm numb.

January, 2011

"A New Year"

Here we go into a new year.
New possibilities present themselves.
But I drag the baggage, it has to come
Because I haven't let go of the fear.

I will not put myself down for this
Because I'm working daily to thrive.
Of course my love and trust for God
Assures me, comforts me, I abide.

I tried to rush the healing process.
I thought I couldn't function unless I was whole.
But I know now I'll never be the same
In my heart there's a hole, I confess.

Yes, a hole lies in the middle of my heart.
It's been there and will remain I fear.
But God sees me through the Blood of Christ.
And He can use me even though I'm missing a part.

January, 2011

"Life Returns"

Life returns when we least expect it.
It returns, bit by bit
It returns, feels so flimsy
It returns, wrapped, wanting out
It returns, as a new candle lit
It returns, no one watches
It returns, everything burns
It returns, I had almost quit
It returns, I just stare and sit
It returns, but alas I've no breath to give it.

Life returns when I've given up
Life returns to stop me from dying
Life returns but the pain doesn't stop
Life returns but it resembles what I think of hell
Life returns but whose life is it?

Life returns but I'm 50 years older
Life returns but without my childhood
Life returns with its own set of rules
Life returns but I don't recognize it
Life returns and I laugh in derision
Life returns and I cry uncontrollably
Life returns and I'm trapped in it all
Life returns, what do I do now?

January, 2011

"What To Do"

I'm angry but I don't know what to do
As a child I just kept my mouth shut.
The more I talked, the worse it got
So I clammed up and it churned in my gut.

Now my heart is swollen with anger
I need to let it out before I burst
It's damaging my love for God
And I'm determined to put Him first.

I'm angry, I'm angry at you
I'm angry at you two.
Neither of you showed me love
But God took over and did what you couldn't do.

January, 2011

"Anger"

It's okay to be angry, it's okay to feel hurt
It's okay to feel sadness too.
It's okay to remember the pain so severe
It's not okay to Ignore that I'm there.

So what do you do when that's someone you adore?
What do you do when It hurts to the core?
You give it to God and leave it there
You give it to Him, for He cares!

January, 2011

"Thirst"

Tomorrow at 3 it's appointment time again
He asks what's happening with me.
I want to tell him nothing's okay
It feels like this day after day.

We'll try to use our entire hour wisely
We'll talk of faith, mercy and trust.
We'll decide what needs to be said first
Or maybe I'll just show my thirst.

My thirst for insides that don't feel dead.
My thirst for days that I keep my head.
My thirst for days with sleep and bed.
My thirst for a time with no dread.
My thirst for a working med.
My thirst for loving words said.
My thirst for Christ, now I'm being Spirit led.

Thank you God!

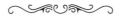

January, 2011

"Recovery"

I can feel the touch of God healing me
I have finally realized pride was the key.
The key to unlocking and releasing the poison
Pride that I was betrayed and tricked, I now see.

I couldn't figure out why I was so angry
I had worked through it, from him to be free.
I had been angry with God for not saving me
I had even been angry at others including me.

Then today I realized it was pride, my control had been snatched.
Pride that my self confidence had been trashed
Pride that my selfishness had suddenly crashed.
It had all been exposed, I was unleashed.

I can now put my trust in God and rest
I'd tried to do all the work; now I'm in his care.
Yep, in the nest and under his wings I'll dwell
That's the safest place to stay, and it's the best!

Trust can only come when pride has been banished
Selfishness interfered with my ability to let go.
Controlling my own life, boy what a mistake!
But now, I'm on the right track, God, You're the only way!

January, 2011

"Ya'll"

Some said I was an accident and never wanted.
Others just stood aside and taunted.
He, well…he took all I had so precious.
But God knew it all, and it was me He protected.

You took the little girl, and did with her as you wanted.
Then you walked off and left her feeling haunted.
You stayed away so long she felt no endearment
But all the while God showered her with His great love.

The breakdown last year sent me into depression
Enemy, you thought this was great and would last forever.
But in that locked hospital room God came and rescued me
Just the opposite of what you wanted to happen.

January, 2011

"He Knows"

God knows what you did
The enemy intended to ruin me.
But when God's presence is working
He turns the ugliness into beauty!

God knows how the abuse hurt me
The complete disregard for this baby.
But He buried the events til I could hear them
The timing is right now maybe.

God knows I was ready to remember
At just the right time I could see.
I was hurt, I was sad, I was damaged
But each moment of the day God was with me.

I'm still searching but I trust God fully
I'm taking it day by day.
I've made it through days by praying often
I'm so sure God is the way.

God knows I want to abide with Him
I'm anxious to let Him take over.
I've tried to correct it on my own
Now I've discovered through Him I'll recover.

January, 2011

"*Love*"

I Love God, yes, my King
I trust God, yes, He makes me sing.
I uplift God, yes, He's the best
I grab hold of God, yes, He stands the test.

I depend on God to lead my life.
I cry out to God to heal my strife.
I look up to God to cover with wings.
I open up to God to hear Him sing.

I give up my pride, please take it Lord,
I give up my anger, there may be more,
If it comes up again, please stop the roar.
I give up my self will, to the very core.

Love, trust, dependence, and His will
This is what I realized tonight.
Pride, anger, self will and doubt
This is what I gave up . . . the fight.

January, 2011

"What I've Learned"

I've learned that when all was taken from me, God was there.

I've learned when those around me didn't love me, God was there.

I've learned that when he used me all up, God was there.

I've learned that when I thought I was nothing, God was there.

I've learned that there has never been a time that God
has not been there.

I've learned that there will never be a time when
God will not be there.

I've learned that He is everything and He can guide me
the rest of the way.

I've learned that He has a future for me and He will be there
every step of the way.

January, 2011

"Through God"

My anger is subsiding; it is thru God's amazing grace.
My love is increasing; it is thru the mercy of God.
My trust is being built; it is through the consistency of God.
My forgiveness is being formed; it is through the example of God.
My hope in the future is appearing; it is through the
longsuffering of God.
My love for God is sweeter; it is through the spread of
His wings over me.

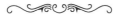

January, 2011

"Trust"

When trust takes hold, all else must run.
When trust arrives the enemy is done.
When I let go of me and my way, God can come.
When trust is allowed the enemy is done.

When anger fills my life, there's no room for God.
It strangles and chokes my ability to grow.
It tells me the lie that I have the right to control.
But tonight, Praise God, I know whose hand I hold.

It's God, It's God, It's my precious longsuffering God.
It's truth, It's truth, It's truth that I've been freed.
It's trust, It's trust, It's trust in God alone.
It's freedom, It's freedom, a feeling I've never known.

January, 2011

"Right On Time"

God, I worried so much about the time I've lost,
Being hurt and angry, depressed and unwell.
I wanted to hurry, to fix whatever the cost
But all the while I forgot with You to dwell.

The pride, the anger, the resentment surprised me.
I was so busy blaming others, and the enemy
That I didn't realize I had tried to handle things, you see
And pushed God to the side refusing to let Him be.

To be what-the answer to all my prayers
To be what-the hero of all my battles
To be what-the end of all my cares
To be what-the Savior of all my snares.

When all the time, all I had to do was reach for You!

January, 2011

"Depression Alas"

Deeper than I've ever been
Every thought gone from my brain
Pressed down to the depths of my soul
Reaching up but unable to crawl out.
Even when I try to forget, it stays.
Sad, so sad, never the same again
Sigh, sigh there's nothing left to say.
I feel as though I'll never be the same.
Only deeper, lower, sadder here I go
Never reaching high enough to get up out of here.

January, 2011

"Pride"

Pity, pity all your time on yourself.
Reaching up above all else, what a joke
In no wise wanting to continue on this way.
Depending upon you, God, please, oh please!
Eagerly I wait for you, I'm nothing on my own.

" Anger "

Aloud I say sweet nothings but inside I scream and shout
Never able to control the pain I feel in my heart.
Going along as normally as my head allows.
Except within myself there's a battle for my soul
Reach out, dear God, reach out for me and never let me go.

"Resentment"

Remembering, regretting, reeling
Everything hurts, everything stings.
Sobbing, screaming, searching for peace
Endless bitterness, despair and grief
Never able to climb out of this mess.
Totally, timelessly God come to me
My soul, my heart, my head waits for You.
Eager for you to touch me and bring me out
Never to fall into the enemy's trap again.
To You, dear God, I give it all to you.

January, 2011

"I Give It to You"

I just said in a poem that I gave it all to You.
I truly meant to hand it off this time
Your Word promises You will never leave me
You only ask that I give it all to You.

Proverbs tells me "lean not unto thine own understanding"
I really need to take that to heart.
So dear, sweet God hear me now
I love you with every part!

January, 2011

"Life is Good"

Life is good, life is rich
When you give yourself to God.
He takes tragedy and pain
And makes it worthwhile to live again.

I thought my life was ruined and gone
I'd given up the idea of even going on.
I had taken my life in my own hands
But I had neglected to notice God's plan.

For you see there never was a time
When God didn't have me on His mind.
He covered me and kept me under His wings
He protected me and guided me as King of Kings.

Even though I didn't have what I needed in those days
The ones who would always treat me right.
I had my dear precious Savior there
Who kept me every day in His loving care.

January, 2011

"God is So Good"

Every night we watch T.V. shows
That just seem to have bits of my woes.
They mention them or show them nonchalantly
But each time I see them I'm left to suppose.

To suppose how many little kids get hurt.
To suppose how many feel like dirt.
To suppose how lost their lives become.
To suppose if they're ever the same again.

I can tell you for sure they're never the same.
I can tell you they wonder what went wrong.
I can tell you the void never goes away.
I can tell you only God can heal you again.

For I know what it's like; I've been there you see.
I've pondered why they couldn't love me.
I tried so hard to do what they wanted
But it just wasn't ever going to get any better.

That is until God revealed the unknown to me
He gently showed me what had been and could be.
He quietly and surely showed me His word
He assured me He had never ever left me alone.

AND HE NEVER WILL! PRAISE GOD!

January, 2011

"Get It Out Of Me"

I've written some poems and a story too
To try to come to terms with what I've been through.
I've even filled ten or eleven journals now;
Trying to help me live through this matter somehow.

The writings have helped, they get it out of me.
The details written down to look back and see.
To look one more time and to know it really happened
To see once again the door that's been opened.

If I could go back and not remember a thing
I think I would go for it, I'd take away the sting.
But the doctor says it would've come out some time
I'd still have been left with the need to reclaim.

So thank you God for staying with me.
For going before me, for helping me see.
For protecting and guiding me all of the way
For helping me learn how to face another day.

January, 2011

"Days"

Good days, bad days,
High days, low days.

Abuse days, healing days,
Ruined days, restored days.

Enemy run days, God honored days,
Defeat days, Victory days.

Despair days, Hope days,
Grace days, Mercy days,
Trust days, Triumph days!

The enemy loses days, God wins and wins and wins days!
Hurray, hurray, hurray, hurray, hurray, hurray, hurray days!